The Beautiful Not Yet
Poems, Essays and Lyrics

By Carrie Newcomer

The Beautiful Not Yet
Poems, Essays and Lyrics

All songs ©2016 Carrie Newcomer Music (BMI)
Administered by BMG Chrysalis

Lyrics for the song "The Beautiful Not Yet" co-written by Chloe Grace

ISBN 978-0-692-76090-1

Cover artwork and design by Hugh Syme
Back cover photo by Jim Krause
Edited by Cate Whetzel
Inside book design by Tim Gaskins

Dedicated to my father, James B. Newcomer

Contents

- Poetry -

- Essays -

- Lyrics -

- Acknowledgements -

Introduction

This book was written between 2014 and 2016. Many of the pieces presented in this collection were the starting point for songs recorded on my album The Beautiful Not Yet, released September 2016. Also included in this collection are the complete lyrics for the songs on The Beautiful Not Yet. I hope you enjoy this companion collection of poetry, essays and lyrics.

Carrie Newcomer
September 2016

- Poetry -

The Beautiful Not Yet

Spring is coming.
Soon,
But not yet.
After the snow,
Before the buds,
Before the blooms,
The world trembles
And vibrates
With muddy possibility.
In a world of doing and things to be done,
What a wonder to walk
In the almost and near,
Here in the beautiful not yet.

Cups of Light

You always arrive bringing light.
Carried in chipped pitchers,
And dented buckets,
Sloshing all that luminous liquid
Out like soapy water
Washing down the muddy floorboards
Of my weary or worried days.

Yes, there were others,
The ones who came carrying
Jars full of shadows
Which are also a kind of gift
I suppose.

But you (my friend)
You always
Always
Arrive bringing dawn.
You open the windows,
Repair the screen door,
Without fanfare,
Or agenda,
Pour out and share
Cups full of light.
And when I am most dry,
You let me drink it all down,
Wiping my thirsty soul
With the back of a grateful hand.

A Question is a Curious Animal

A question is truly a curious animal,
An elegant doe that peers from the shadows,
A bird that calls and does not call again.
There are questions you circle like a beast with sharp horns,
Keeping track of it in glimpses from the corner of your eye.
There are questions you did not want or see coming,
A stampede of horses knocking you to the ground,
Where you pant and wipe your eyes in the billowing dust.
Some questions are like babies placed in unpracticed arms,
Arms that feel too clumsy to hold
Such a strange, perfect thing.

There are questions that keep us incarnate and restless,
Luminous and now as the brief Luna moth.
There are ones that invite us inward and outward,
Like a light in the distance,
Or the crystalline lines
Of a singular snowflake
Riding for a while on a wolf's winter back.

There are questions with no answers,
Answers never the point,
Just an owl-like enigma gliding in from the dark
Whispering "Who? "I wonder"
And "Why?"
There are questions that abide deep under the ground,
Resting like field mice, who sleep with no shame,
Because some kinds of growth only happens with time,
In the safe, quiet rooms
Of the soft, secret heart.

Some questions we ask and then ask again,
Exploring the places where the boundaries have changed,
The ones you thought that you'd answered a long time ago,
And yet they come yowling, a stray cat at the window.
A dog that keeps nudging, eyes trained on the door.

A question is truly a curious animal,
Sure footed and shy, fierce and untamed,
It wades in the river where the mist meets the water,
Brown eyes gazing from beneath lowered lashes,
With a cry like a brilliant startle of wings.

Saturday Morning Market

I am awash with a deep abiding love
For shiny purple eggplants,
Real and rounded in such womanly ways.
I am beside myself with wonder
At the many shapes and hues
Of crook-necked squash and new potatoes,
Earthy red and ochre tan,
Goldfinch yellow and deep summer green.
I am grateful to tears
For fresh beet greens and rhubarb,
Green peppers and Swiss chard,
And for the first vine-ripe tomatoes
That are so perfect you go ahead
And eat one like an apple,
Leaning forward
Without looking
To see if anyone is watching.
I am blessing the names
Of the farmers and bread bakers,
Sunburnt and beautiful,
Freckled and friendly,
Who make change
And comfortable conversation.

This is real abundance
Of the senses and spirit,
A true kind of church,
With its arms open wide
To the eaters and eaten,
The growers and grown,

To all who come looking
For what is common and earthly,
Luminous and lasting,
And to be dumbstruck with wonder
By what we carry back home
In an ordinary basket.

A Shovel is a Prayer

A shovel is a prayer to the farmer's foot,
When she steps down and the soft earth gives way.
A book is a prayer when the words call the reader,
When the story is water to a spirit that's thirsty,
Which is unlike the prayer that is doggish and faithful,
Eyes trained on the door where the beloved returns.
A friend is a prayer when they ask the right question,
When they bring over soup,
And they laugh at your jokes,
When they text you a photo,
Because you are lonely
Or weary
Or just that far from home.

A fish is a prayer
To a man in a boat
Sunburnt and shading his eyes,
Who drops in his line,
And tracks its descent,
Down below the surface of things.
Which is almost, but not quite,
Like the prayer of the fish,
Letting go of what's safe,
In a litany of leaping,
Just for a glimpse,
Of what is glowing and glorious,
So close,
But still out of reach.

A glove is a prayer that covers the hand,

It's a dancer with taped feet and toes.
A poem is prayer when it hints at the edges,
Says more than it says,
Or points to what's true.
A baby is a prayer when its finally asleep,
A whispered "Amen" at the end of the day.
It is the dome of the sky all scattered with stars
Bearing names we don't know,
Which makes us feel haunted.
It's heavy as grief and weightless as smoke,
A dam that keeps breaking
Washing down the dry valleys,
Carving out canyons of stone.

Breathless

Riding my bike down a narrow country road,
On one side a dense forest,
On the other a wide dusky meadow.
And suddenly beside me,
A graceful young doe
Was bounding in beautiful unhurried leaps.
And just for a moment
We were moving together,
Brown limbed and strong,
In the blue evening light.
And then with a burst of beautiful speed
She dashed across the road,
And disappeared into the woods,
Leaving me breathless
With a feeling of visitation,
Of Holy Communion,
Like I'd been touched
Ever so briefly,
By something wild and completely unbroken.

And ever since that evening,
The world has felt less weary.
And I've felt surer of the promise,
That what I do not know,
Or might not see coming,
Could leap out in unexpected glory,
At any given moment.

Miracles

There are so many of them,
I start to lose count.
There are too many to hold in my two hands.
So I just keep dropping them like acorns
Into a basket hiked up on my hip.

The revelation of light, filtered through rain,
A sky so pregnant it weeps with the joy of it.
The circular wonder
Of a big bite of darkness
That keeps chasing and catching
And releasing the moon.

Not to mention all the ordinary magic,
That cat will be cat
And dog will be dog
And chickens will do
Pretty much what chickens have always done.

In addition to the miracles that are brief and strange,
A flash of blue from the corner of the eye.
Or the bare and beautiful confession we missed
When checking our email on the sly.

All these and more,
Day after day,
Another acorn in the basket
Another stone in the water
Sending out ripples
Across the evening pond.

What Is Heavy Turns to Spirit

All that is hard and heavy turns to spirit.
It cannot help but eventually
Become like a cup of ink
That is poured out into the ocean.
I do not doubt that for a time
The ink darkens the water,
Obscures and displaces the light,
Leaching out its tendrils
Staining what it touches.
But eventually,
Finally,
The ink must break down into its smallest elements,
And even the stains become only faint shadows
Barely noticeable to the outer eye.

This does not belittle the awful impact of a cup full of shadow.
It is only to say, that in an ocean of goodness,
In an expanse of health and light,
A cup full of dark can only prevail for so long,
Until it is overcome and transformed back into spirit,
Back into its smallest elements,
Received into the body,
To be made whole
And healed.

To Be Like a Tree

See how the trees
Reach up and outward
As if their entire existence
Were an elegant gesture of prayer.
See how they welcome the breath of spirit,
In all its visible and invisible forms.
See how the roots reach downward and out,
Embracing the physical,
The body and bones
Of its earth and stone soul,
Allowing half of its life to be sheltered
In the most quiet and secret places.

Oh, if I could be more like a tree,
To feel the breath of invisible spirit
Touch me as tenderly as a kiss on the forehead.
If I could courageously and confidently
Dig down into the dark
Where the ground water runs deep,
Where shelter and sanctuary
Can be had and held.

Ah, to be like a tree
With all its bent and unbent places,
A whole and holy thing
From its topmost twigs
To its deepest taproot
To all the good and graceful
Spaces between.

Typewriters

I learned to type on my father's old Royal Deluxe,
A reliable heavy-as-hell 1940's manual.
I remember the ratcheting sound as you rolled in the paper,
The snap and tap of the type bars as they hit,
The little square type guide and the mechanical movements
Of the ribbon as it lowered and raised.

On my father's Royal you had to hit the keys hard.
Pre-electric typing was not for timid fingers.
I recall the pleasing you're-almost-there bell,
That rang when you neared the right margin,
And the satisfying whack and thunk of the manual return
That would shake our red kitchen table.

I like having spell check and easy editing functions.
I don't think I could ever hit return,
Or roll back that page completely.
But I do miss a workspace without several modes of distraction,
Alerts and prompts and open applications,
All vying for my attention as I write.

I miss a world when you did one thing
And then you did the next.
I miss the physical rhythm of moving thoughts and ideas
Into words and sentences.
I miss how I stopped when the arms jammed,
Or the ribbon wore out,
Or the Liquid Paper needed to dry,
Creating a pause,
A break from the headlong,

My mind coming up for air and perspective.
I miss my comfortable relationship with imperfection.
That the ink was never completely smooth,
And that it had a tendency to be thicker
Or thinner on certain letters.
Our current world is becoming less tolerant of blemish.
These days, we hear only recorded voices that are perfectly pitched,
And see images that have been computer corrected.
Perfect skin, teeth, shaved waistlines and enhanced eye color.
We see only news anchors and actresses who have been surgically
sculpted
To fit more acceptable standards of youth and beauty.
And hardest of all,
We now expect children
Never to be uncertain,
To perform perfectly,
On tests that only measure
The perfectly measurable.

But not so long ago,
The humble typewriter was a daily reminder
Of how to be in relationship,
With a letter that always sticks,
And a bell that keeps you from going totally over the edge,
And that interesting things happen during an unexpected pause,
And that even the fastest most capable typist,
Occasionally has to pull out a page,
Crumple it up,
And start again.

Blessing

May you wake with a sense of play,
An exultation of the possible.
May you rest without guilt,
Satisfied at the end of a day well done.
May all the rough edges be smoothed,
If to smooth is to heal,
And the edges be left rough,
When the unpolished is more true
And infinitely more interesting.
May you wear your years like a well-tailored coat
Or a brave sassy scarf.
May every year yet to come:
Be one more bright button
Sewn on a hat you wear at a tilt.
May the friendships you've sown
Grown tall as summer corn.
And the things you've left behind,
Rest quietly in the unchangeable past.
May you embrace this day,
Not just as any old day,
But as this day.
Your day.
Held in trust
By you,
In a singular place,
Called now.

Before I Knew to Look

Often it is the fine detail,
A small thing,
That snaps me back into the here and now.
Amber light coming through the trees,
The slippery soft sound of creek water,
Running beneath a tender filigree of ice,
Ella-Bear my mutt dog rolling in the fresh snow,
The give and chop of a carrot on the cutting board,
The image of two grown men,
Wiping tears of laughter
From the crinkled edges of their eyes.

It is as easy to be lost,
As it is hard to be lost.
But am growing bored with tomorrow,
With what will be, and how I will be then,
Weary of worried speculation or detached dreaming,
Which are phantoms only,
The flip side of creative imagining.

I am happiest these days
When yesterday is an old friend
With whom I share much history.
And tomorrow is willing to wait,
For its own time above the horizon line.

I am most content now
When I hold my own life,
Right here, in the bowl of my cupped hands,
And sense that the hollow spaces

Are actually filled with Light,
Light that was already there,
Before I knew to look.

The Hummingbird

This morning,
A bottle green hummingbird
Hovered...
Its tiny extraordinary wings,
A blur of determined motion.
It hung there,
Surveying
A bright stand of bee balm
With blossoms tender as skin,
Red as summer berries.
It paused,
Waited,
As if it were gathering up its chutzpah.
And then in a whistle, it barged in like a cowboy
Pushing through the saloon doors
Audaciously ordering a sweet sarsaparilla,
With a straw.
It then ruffled and rumpled,
Tasted and tested,
And then with an incomprehensible dazzle of feathers,
(All the bumblebees whispering,
"Who was that masked man?")
It was gone,
The saloon door still swinging,
All the straw wrappers skittering,
Floating,
Ever so lightly,
To the ground.

The Knitting Shoppe

I finger the yarn,
Checking its strength and quality,
Comparing the weights and colors.
The shop keeper watches me,
Unsure and unconvinced.
I am a foreign woman in a foreign land,
Possessing only the barest words of her language.

I pick up a particularly beautiful skein.
It is soft and obviously hand-dyed.
And sighing the sigh of true appreciation
I meet her eyes and breathe,
"sehr schön"
"Very lovely."

She stops,
Then beams,
Proud that the quality
Of the material she loves
Transcends.

We nod in agreement
As women (and knitters) will sometimes do,
With shared understanding
Of the humble importance
Of simple
Useful things
Which can only be created
One stitch at a time.

The Gunflint Trail

We are now entering radio silence.
No cell phone reception.
No white noise.
Leaving every buffeting thing,
Driving true north.

Sentinels of pines and birch
Stand in quiet witness.
Whole gatherings of cattail,
That nod and consider
The hush of the car wheels
As we pass.
The narrow road ahead
Reaches out and beyond,
Into the wild wooded distance,
As perfect as the pictures
They used to print on church fans.

At a deserted turn out,
We stop the car,
Pause,
and rest.

And there,
At the edge of the water,
Is a silence so deep,
It comes up from the ground
And enters through your feet.
It is a quiet that happens in your body
And not just your ears,

A silence that is
So exactly what it is,
That you must come into its presence
On your knees,
If at all.

Aftershock, the Second Violence

There is the first violence,
The flash of light,
The hammer falls,
A wail spirals into the sky.
Our eyes fill and spill,
In a human solidarity of suffering.

Then the sharp-toothed sharks gather,
FOX, CNN, MSNBC, ABC, CBS, NBC,
My God, even PBS.
They feed on tragedy from a pot furiously stirred,
Cooked up with conflict, salaciously salted,
Tasting only of fear.
The ugly fringed edges of opinion
Are given equal time,
And therefore equal weight.
The first violence is breathtaking and terrible.
And yet, the best in us reaches out,
Our hearts softened to one another,
This was somebody's
Mother or
Brother or
Child.

The second violence is stone cold
As tragedy becomes commodity,
When suffering sells,
When this cycle features
24/7 of drum beating and seam ripping,
With no attempt to explore or embrace

What might really heal what's been wounded,
Or mend what's been torn.

Zero Gravity Flying

It is deeply disorienting to begin in one ecosystem
And a few hours later, land miles from where I began.
In the time it takes to drink a cup of weak coffee,
You can cross great divides and wide empty places.
You can skip over deep canyons and waterless deserts.
You can hurtle above all obstacles
Instead of finding true passage.
And always,
Every time I step out into the terminal,
I stand motionless for a moment, blinking and confused.
My small mammal brain shouts with concern,
"We do not have wings.
We cannot fly in this manner without incurring the wrath
Of all the nameless bird gods."
Really, I think that.

A human-size journey should be more humanly paced.
It took me years to learn to play the guitar.
How many hours did I sit alone in my room,
Working those sharp silver strings,
Until my fingertips bled,
Until my hands knew the shapes by heart?

It took most of my childhood to learn what children must learn,
And all the years after to unlearn a good deal of the same,
Keeping the grain and tossing the chaff.
It took me forever to finally forgive
What I knew I could never forget,
And to understand that the outcome
Of reaching and wanting

Is usually to only want more.
It took multiple times in multiple forms,
Different incarnations of the very same lesson,
Until in a blinding flash of the obvious,
I saw what was common to all of that trouble,
Had always, always been me.

On a human-sized journey you have to get lost,
Double back and blunder around in the dark,
And accepting the knowledge that there is rarely a clear path,
But sometimes,
Just sometimes,
There is a true north,
Or a well-lighted sign that miraculously points,
Somewhere in the right general direction.

Air-travel feels like cheating,
The illusion of zero gravity,
A magician's sleight of hand,
A comfortable distraction,
From the knowledge that true journeys
Cannot be avoided,
But must always be taken,
In time and in the body,
As well as the soul.

A Circle of Seasons (From Betty's Diner: The Musical)

This is a cycle of poems that were written for Betty's Diner: The Musical

I.
Now is the season of extravagance.
When the world is deep green and generous,
When the warm air grows thick
And every shady place becomes a sanctuary.
Spring blew us a kiss
With a promise to return,
Allowing summer to open its arms
With a wide rakish grin.

No, July is not subtle.
It is full to the brim,
Spilling over
With dazzling Light.

II.
August is the threshold.
Between summer and fall,
The days are still long
With endless heat.
Our sleep is restless,
And even light sheets
Are tossed aside.

And yet,
In the drugstores
Are displays of anticipation

As parents buy their children
Notebooks and pencils,
Lunch boxes and paints,
Scissors with no sharp edges.

Now is the time
When we sense a true thing,
That the wheel keeps on turning
Without pretense or pause,
And ready or not
The question keeps calling,
Droning and determined,
Rising like the circular sound
Of cicadas in chorus.

III.
This is how we love
In the golden light of autumn.
We know what is coming
And so we walk further
And longer
Just to feel it and live it,
And take it
Completely and joyously
Into our hearts.

But let go we must
Although we resist,
As surely as each leaf
Bids farewell to the branch,
Launching and lifting
Into the air.

IV.

Late autumn is the season
Of abundance and loss,
The harvest comes in,
The gardens are made ready.
The nights are getting longer,
And every day the leaves fall
Like so many golden coins.

But this loss does not feel
Like the wailings of grief.
It is more like the final notes
Of beautiful song,
When we lean into the ache
Of those last vibrations,
Our hearts broken open,
Empty hands reaching
As the sound fades
Into soft memory.

The dark nights are coming,
But they are not here yet.
So let us be grateful
For what was and what is,
For the air filled with rain
And dust
And the circling descent
Of fire colored leaves.

V.

It is the season of mercy,
The season of memory,
At the end of December,

At the turn of the year
When our spirits go quiet
And we turn toward each other
For company and kindness
Which is honest and human
And softens the hardest of things.

And perhaps that's the reason
We are all here,
To be a safe place to launch
And a soft place to land,
To murmur at night
And to notice a miracle
Pushing up through the sidewalk
And to recognize love
In all its various
And unexpected
Forms.

VI.
Winter is the oldest season.
It is easy to believe that nothing is happening
When the ground is bare or blanketed with snow.
But quietly below the surface
A seed has been dreaming,
Gathering courage into its secret heart.
How often we are surprised the world goes green
All at once and seemingly overnight.
Because we did not see
The moment of quickening
When the seed was awakened
And unobserved began its journey
Reaching up toward the light.

And so we are amazed and a little astonished
When the shoot breaks through
The muddy spring ground
Deliberately unfolding,
Taking on the shape
Of a question mark.

VII.
A new spring enters,
The keeper of a promise,
The season that always returns.
She carries in her basket
Wildflowers and strawberries,
This year's fruit
From last year's seeds.

Yes, there are questions,
And occasionally answers,
The simple ones,
The most important ones,
That cannot be approached
Or even seen,
Until we go out looking
For something else entirely,
Following the hunch to its natural end.
Only then can we return
To where we began,
Grateful and humbled
By what the world has poured in,
And all that we have poured out,

Yes, friends,
A new life is beginning,

And it is taking up exactly
Where the old life left off.

VIII.
Morning becomes noon,
Becomes night,
Becomes morning again.
That's how we circle the sun.
Each season enters,
Swaggers, shines
And surrenders,
Pouring itself out
Into the waiting cup of the next.

Although there's a sense
Of rightness and beauty,
When the veil pulls away
It is still a great mystery
How one life passes
As another begins.

So for now
In this moment,
In this luminous moment,
All is well,
And all is as it should be.
For what is lasting and lovely,
All that is humble and holy,
Abides here in our presence,
As we sit side by side,
Gathered as friends,
Gathered as true family.

For Love

When I found out
I thought about her.
Of course,
That was first.
But eventually,
After the quiet conversation,
And the promises and assurances,
And best-case scenarios,
After we'd murmured and cradled the knowledge,
That they can do so much more now
Than what they could do for our mothers,
After we sighed and said, "I love you"
And the phone went blank,
I thought about myself.
Selfish I know,
But human.

I clenched my fist and closed my eyes.
I paced the floor and tore up paper.
Whispering so as not to howl out the words.
There are too many now,
An entire expanding cloud of beloved souls
Who fought valiantly and courageously
But eventually lost.
Lost their hair.
Lost weight.
Lost so many shining and unused years.

In that moment I tried to remember
How to breathe,

How to pray,
How to believe that there is no callous God,
Or bored God-like person,
Capriciously doling out sorrow,
Dumping punishment or pain,
For any purpose under heaven.
You see, a disease is a disease,
Impersonal and indiscriminate.
The hundred year flood
Sweeping away all who just happened
To get in the way.
You see, it does no good,
No good at all
To rail in righteous indignation
Or to vent my bewildered bone-shaking fury
At the curious connecting tissue of the universe,
To roar and rage at what holds all things together,
Even when they are falling apart.

And so the healing begins
And the first miracle happens.
In the calm space after a good cry
I let go of me.
I unclench my hands,
Returning to love,
To what must always be done,
For love.

On a Train from Hannover to Berlin

This poem is where the song "The Season of Mercy" began.

Traveling east,
Tall straight pines and ghost-white birch,
That stand like sentries lining the rails,
Closing in and opening out into wide green pastures.
We pass houses with steeply pitched red tile roofs.
A lone blue kite hangs in the distance,
Someone I cannot see tethering it to the ground.
There are unfamiliar sounds of an unfamiliar language
Creating the bubble of quiet that happens
When the room is filled to overflowing with
Unrecognizable words.
I cannot speak even the smallest courtesies
Which feels like losing a basic framework
I use to recognize myself.

In this country the door locks click perfectly,
Nothing rattles or wobbles,
And there is usually good bread and cheese
Somewhere to be found.
An impossibly blond woman sits
With her impossibly blond little girl
Totally unaware of their own impossible wattage.
They are sitting next to an African man,
Earbuds in, singing loudly and completely off-key,
While young men in the bar car
Are drinking and laughing,
Posturing as young men will do.
Two dark-eyed children gaze at me
From beneath dark eyelashes,

A faint smile
From the smallest corners of the girl's beautiful mouth
Given to me, the woman
Who noticed and smiled back.

All is strange here and yet, helplessly familiar-
Wide November fields, the hay baled into rolls,
Everything amber and done for the year.
The dusty white and blue-gray cumulus clouds
Seen from the bottom, beams of light escaping
Spilling out like marbles on a tile floor.

I turn to my traveling companion,
A man who for so many years
Has followed his guitar
Like a flashlight in the dark.
We speak in comfortable, quiet conversation
About the nuance of language
Spoken and unspoken.
We are sensing the music
That somewhere between us
Hangs suspended and expectant,
Felt but yet unformed,
Just waiting
As it always does
For the open container
Of the perfect moment.

Flat Tire

It's a long wide stretch from Louisville to Indianapolis.
I was driving in my ancient Honda
The odometer clicking away
Well within range of unreliable.
I was traveling with a friend,
We were talking about politics,
Lamenting the loss of civility,
Describing our despair,
And the ever widening chasm
Of our hopelessly divided world.

Then somewhere between a string of small rural towns,
My tire began to make that stomach dropping
Flopping noise, that sounds like
Flat, flat, flat.
Miraculously, a sign announced just ahead,
A garage for commercial trucks.
We limped off the highway into a dusty parking lot
Completely lined with stacks of huge semi tires,
Knowing that most likely there would be no help for me here.
But every now and then
Necessity or circumstance will force your hand,
Will leave you no other choice
But to give it a Last-Chance-Texaco try.

A mechanic emerged out of the enormous mouth of the garage,
Wearing oil soaked overalls, a blond stubble and a sunburnt face,
An American flag pin tacked to his camouflage baseball cap,
Big hands strong enough to budge a stubborn lug nut,
And most certainly an NRA card in his wallet.

He took in the scene,
The flat tire,
The guitars piled in the back,
The "War Is Not the Answer" bumper sticker.
He looked at me,
He looked at my friend,
And I just knew,
That somehow he knew,
I was a registered Democrat,
Traveling with a gay theologian,
In a foreign-made car,
With an eco-coffee mug in the cup holder.
We were of different tribes.
All the signs were there,
The team jerseys and war paint
Calling our code words
Across the great divide.
I said, "It appears this garage is for commercial trucks,
But can you help?"
He just gestured at the garage,
No hint of a smile,
And said, "Yup."
I gave him the keys.

For the next 20 minutes,
My friend and I wandered around the office,
Which smelled of burnt coffee and transmission fluid.
We kept looking at one another whispering
"Do you think he saw the bumper "sticker?"
"Do you think this is going to cost an arm and leg?"
"Do you think he has a gun rack on his truck?"

Eventually my car pulled up to the office,
And our monosyllabic mechanic got out.
He nodded and said,
"Fixed."
That's it,
"Fixed."
I nodded back. "Thank you, that's great.
How much do I owe you?"
He smiled (only in his eyes).
"Naw, it dint take long."

So we climbed into our twice-blessed car.
Our new best friend in camouflage and coveralls
Touched the tip of his cap,
Turned, and disappeared,
Like a holy man,
Into the dark cave of the truck garage.
"Never assume," I said.
"It is all still possible," my friend answered.

It is true. We still live
In a world of unvarnished kindness,
Of unearned and unexpected grace.
And the pervasive myth of nothing-much-in-common
Is dispelled on a daily basis.
Distrust can be changed and averted
By relationship and experience,
And hopelessly divided had been entirely transformed
From an unavoidable certainty,
To only a failure of imagination.

Dowsing

It is like dowsing,
This writing of poems and songs.
First, you take a bit of forked willow branch,
Then, you breathe a prayer or incantation over it.
You point it toward the ground and hope it senses water.
You trust the small movements in your hands.
You have to let go of the things people have told you,
Like, "That's impossible." "You will look foolish."
"It is not real." And "You will fail."
You believe in hard work.
You believe in unearned grace.
You sit down on the leaves and let go of finding anything today.

Dowsing is trying again,
Remembering what you learned,
And then forgetting what you learned,
So that you might learn something new.
It is following the hunch,
Trusting where it takes you,
Even into the most haunted or dimly lit places.

Dowsing is practical magic.
It is practical in that it has an earthy goal,
To find and bring forth
What saves and preserves,
Heals or grows.
It is magic because no one can really explain how it works,
Or how to make it happen.
It just does.
And then it doesn't.

So every morning I go out, and pick up my willow branch.
In all kinds of weather and all through the year,
I point its sensitive end out toward the world,
And then turn it back and touch my own heart.
I bless the branch when there's water,
And try not to despair when it's dry.
I keep on dowsing and reaching,
Carefully sensing,
Trusting when an invitation
Turns in my hands.

Floaters

It started with a flash of light,
Seen for a moment at the corner of my eye.
Then a filmy black web descended,
Undulating like seaweed in water,
Obscuring the center of my vision.
Later, an eye doctor,
A young blond woman in a white coat,
Said, "This is permanent" and "This is early, but a common process of
aging."
It is called a floater, and it is completely normal.
Nothing can be done.
Nothing could have prevented it.
She speaks these words as if they might be comforting,
As if this would allow me to sit back in my early (but not that early)
dotage,
Fold my hands over my belly like a Buddha,
And nod my head like something tamed and agreeable.

I will never again, with blissfully ignorant clarity,
Gaze at the chill October moon,
Delight at April light streaming through new leaves,
Or see stones and sky at the same time in a summer stream,
I will not see the beautiful planes of your face,
Or hay rolls in the fields made luminous at sunset.
I will never again see these things I love,
That thrill and inspire me,
And more often than anything else,
Remind me that I am mysteriously and completely
Connected to Light,
Without a moving shadow,

An ugly black web,
First in my field of vision.

For an artist, for a poet,
This is loss,
This is blinding grief.
My eyes well up with tears,
And bewildered questions,
Which I fight to keep from spilling over my bottom lid.
The young doctor sees my distress (without black webs before her
eyes),
And smiles the smile you give a sweet old dog,
And says, "You'll get used to it."
And in my mind I say (in a not sweet old dog way),
"To hell with you and your white coat,
To hell with these floaters."
But, instead, I take the Xeroxed information sheet,
I pay my bill, and walk out into a fractured parking lot,
In a fractured world, with a fractured sky.
And for the very first time in my life,
I encounter age,
Not like a glove that gets worn,
But still feels like yours,
But like a blunt hammer,
Sure, condescending,
And utterly impersonal.

The Presence of Absence

There is a hole in the place you used to be.
Sometimes it fades
Like an ink stain or memory,
Or a word on the tip of your tongue.
Sometimes it yawns open like a crumbling pothole
Deep enough to take out a tire,
That strands me by the side of the road,
My hands uselessly dangling,
Watching but not participating
In the endlessly moving
Unconscious river
Of the working world.

I can pinpoint the moment,
The shock and grief,
The unwanted truth
That the world will pretty much go on
Without you,
And in turn
Without me.
And ever since then
This hollowed out place has become a companion,
A consort and confederate,
The partner I did not choose.
For better and for worse
To have and to hold,
World without end,
Amen.

Foolish

When I was a girl
I told my father
"In class today I didn't ask a question."
He looked at me and inquired "Why was that?"
And I said, "I didn't want to look foolish
Or simple
Or stupid."
"Ah," he said, "But, the one who never asks
Is the one who never learns.
Who is the wiser
In the long run?"

And that was the day I gave up
Any attempt to appear sly
Or be as guarded as a closed book,
And began to live like
An open one.

Kindness

Kindness is human size,
Honest and doable,
Softening even the hardest of days,
The country cousin to love,
Unpretentious,
And daily,
And completely possible.
It takes out its earbuds
And listens to your story.
It gives up its seat on the bus
And hums in the kitchen,
Washing dishes when nobody asked it to.

And more often than not,
If I start with a little kindness
Love is usually following
Just a few steps behind,
Nodding and smiling
And saying,
"That's the way it's done."
"Yes, honey,
That's the way it is done."

Impossible

"Impossible," she said. "It can't be done."
"Why not?" I asked.
She looked across her desk at me,
"Because you have to be able to measure a thing to know if you've succeeded.
You can't just heft a rock in your hand and say it's heavy.
You have to weigh it properly and write it down."
I tried to explain,
"But not everything can be measured in weights and numbers.
How does one measure the beauty of the light on the pond?
Or the value of lightning bugs flashing their undecipherable Morse code?
How does one assess the wisps of a dream
That has left you with the lingering feeling
Of having spoken with someone you loved and lost?"
She pushed her fashionable eyeglasses up her powdered nose and sighed.
"Oh, you're one of those."

She leaned back, crossed her legs and said,
"Listen, I don't want any trouble here."
She caught my silent expression.
"Just turn in your results or I'll have to mark you down as a no show."
I decided to give it one more try.
"We are swimming in different rivers that lead to different lakes."
She looked at me expectantly and I continued.
"We are not trying to get to the same place,
So what I see along the way will not seem relevant to you."
"Come now," she said, "it's not that hard.
Do you use a mathematical model, stats, questionnaires, focus groups?

Do you float it out on Facebook and calculate the likes and shares and such?"
I knew she wanted equations
And I only had pencil sketches.
She wanted something solid she could hold in her hands or file in a drawer.
I only had the shreds of the song I sang as a child with my mother.
She wanted to cover her ass,
I wanted to throw open my arms to possibility.
So I picked up my drawings of sunlight and Lightning bugs,
I gathered the smooth stones I'd found by the pond,
I shrugged, turned toward the door,
And humming the shreds of that long ago song,
I left the florescent lights of her sharp edged office,
And stepped out
Into a luminous world.

Things I Never Thought I'd Say

My dog has five sweaters.
I don't have to finish every book I start.
In spite of all my mistakes, she turned out just fine.
Living with more questions than answers feels right.
Let's throw some tofu on the grill.
I make my living on the meanderings of my mind.
I can afford the name brand Cheerios, but I stopped eating Cheerios.
I have several longtime friendships that I haven't screwed up.
I found a copperhead snake on my porch and dispatched it with a
shovel.
I miss gathering with friends to listen to both sides of a new album.
I kissed a giraffe.
I don't have to be afraid of that now.
I get a little weepy when I smell Vicks VapoRub
Or Chanel N°5
Mile wide tornados happen regularly.
I know the names of hundreds of wildflowers, trees and bird calls
And yet, there are more to learn,
Which does not feel like a failing,
But a wonderment.
My two lesbian friends are legally married.
I don't have to wear a slip.
It's not my parents' fault.
The most intelligent news on television is presented by late-night
comedians.
They ended the space program.
Our president is an African American.
I don't have to hold my tongue.
I don't have to speak.
I am too old now to die young.

The man I married twenty years ago still surprises me.
My inner teacher can be trusted.
Despite any evidence to the contrary,
It is all still completely possible.

The Slender Thread

This poem is where the song "The Slender Thread" began.

She used to watch me pack my bags.
I knew she was pondering,
Considering,
The kind of kid that takes in everything.
She saw the black dress
And the black jeans
And the black motorcycle boots
The black socks and guitar strings
The credit card machine
The three books of poetry
And a Rand McNally.
She saw me fill up the little bottles
Scrutinizing all I was taking with me
And all that I was leaving behind.
She heard the practical.
"Roll your t-shirts and take an extra toothbrush."
She heard the calming advice,
 "You can always trust a McDonald's bathroom."
She saw what women push against.
"Black creates the illusion of a taller silhouette."
She saw the calendar and map
I taped on the refrigerator,
With all the places I would be,
Every address and phone number,
Carefully marked and charted,
Written in a sturdy script,
So that I would never just be
Gone.
No, no, she could always say,

"The one I love has left this map
A clear itinerary of her movements
Leading from her to me."

And yet, she stayed and I left.
And so there was no way for her to know
The time shift of the road,
When so much happens
And happens intensely,
So that when I returned
There would be that inevitable moment
Of infinite wonder,
And loneliness,
Because everything was pretty much the same,
Everything but me.
She did not see me pull out a little bag,
And carefully arrange
On every cigarette-burnt Motel 6 end table,
My traveling altar,
A feather, a stone,
A folded piece of paper,
And a lock of her hair,
Or see me pack it all up in the morning,
And tuck the bag
Back into my inside coat pocket.
She did not know I was spooling out a slender thread,
Sometimes half way around the world,
Connecting her heart
To mine,
The only sure means,
To find my way home.

- Essays -

Be Kind, Be True, and Pay Attention - Goshen College 2016 Commencement Address

Commencement address by Carrie Newcomer at the 118th Goshen College Commencement on Sunday, April 24, 2016.

Good afternoon, it is a pleasure and honor to be a part of the graduation ceremony of the Goshen College Class of 2016. Thank you, President Jim Brenneman, and the selection committee for the opportunity to speak with you today. As a Goshen College alumna myself, it has been good to have the chance to reflect upon my own time here on this campus, and the powerful ways it changed me, which included experiencing a wider and more diverse world during my Study-Service Term, learning how to fire raku pottery, traveling with a theater troupe, and cleaning six gallons of mashed potatoes off the cafeteria kitchen walls after I pushed the wrong button on the industrial mixer. I admit I was little surprised when I received the invitation to speak to you today. My lifework as a traveling musician and songwriter of hard-to-categorize-spiritual-but-not-religious-music did not show up on the chalkboard as one of the top ten professions on junior high school career day – and it wasn't something that seemed likely to lead me here today. And so, because my vocational path has been a little unusual, the questions I've been asking myself in preparation for today were "What can I offer to a roomful of new graduates who are heading out in so many different directions?" and "What is it about my own story that might be of use or service to you?"

Full disclosure, I can't even count the number of performances and public speaking events I've done in the past 30 years. But, this is my first commencement address. I've written hundreds of songs and poems, but I'd never written a commencement address. So what did I do? I did what many of us do when we feel at a loss or unsure about some new task. I Googled it. You know, "How to write an effective commencement speech." There were all these sites that outlined inspirational topics and important messages for new graduates, like "Follow your Dreams" and "Don't Be Afraid to Fail" and "Take Risks and Embrace Change." There were Amazon links to whole books on commencement speaking, and PDFs of brilliant speeches by famous people like John F. Kennedy, Steve Jobs, Maya Angelou and the Dalai Lama. I clicked around for a while, but pretty quickly I stopped. I stopped because I realized that I didn't want to talk to you about big concepts or abstract ideas. I wanted to focus on small things, human-sized ideas that have made a real difference in my life and work that may be of use to you as well. So here they are, three things that have become important practices and practical guides. "Be true. Be kind. And pay attention." These three things do overlap a bit, but I'll start with "be true." So, what do I mean when I say "be true?" I believe we are all born with affinities, things that we lean into and love just because we do. Two children are born into the same family and they are night and day. How many people here have a sibling? Yes, and they are just like you. No, any parent will tell you that each child is their own little person from the moment they are born. I first encountered this idea in Parker J. Palmer's beautiful book Let Your Life Speak: Listening for the Voice of Vocation, which I recommend for anyone, but especially for you at this point in your life. Think about it. There are activities that have always made you lose track of time. Can you remember the things you loved to do as a child? For some folks, it was the elegance of mathematics, for others it was practicing free throws, or LEGOs, or team sports. For some of us it was reading everything you could get your hands on about bugs or horses or the stars. For some of us it was endlessly putting BAND-AIDs on their dolls or doing dental work on their bears. Think about it, doesn't it just make you happy to remember those things? When I was a kid my favorite game was called, "makin' somethin'." "What are you doing Carrie?" "Makin' somethin'." I was making little songs and stories. I was drawing pictures and making stuff out of paper and glue, leftover fabric or clay. And all these years later, I'm still so happy when I'm makin' something; a song, a story, pumpkin biscuits for my dog, making something, creating something new. There's a clue in these things we naturally love. Sometimes the correlation is pretty direct. My older sister played school every day of her young life, and she's been one of the most passionate educators I've ever known. But sometimes the correlation is poetic. My friend Chris once told me that he really, really loved his job, but that his work had no relationship to what he loved to do as a kid. I asked him what he loved to do as a kid and he described how his family owned a back forty section of woods behind his house. He would spend every day all summer creating winding paths through those woods. He'd make little signs so that people wouldn't lose their way. He even created rest stops so a traveler could take a break to sit and think. I said, "Chris, you're a pastor and vocational reflection counselor—you're still helping people find their way through the woods." He just smiled and said, "Huh. I guess so." You see, we can learn to do a lot of things well. We are human beings with opposable thumbs. But, I believe the closer we get to what we love by nature, when we operate from our truest heart, the more potent our work AND our lives become

But being true is not a destination you arrive at and stop. Being true is an unfolding process; you keep checking in with your heart to see if your inner life is in harmony with your outer circumstances. I know, I know, you're thinking, "but how does this all work, and what does this process look like?" For me, it looked like my own father, a man of deep integrity, who chose to stay true many times in the course of his career and life as an educator, sometimes at a great personal and professional cost. He could not say what he did not believe. He would not stay silent if the truth needed to be spoken. He could not be someone that he was not. My father's example inspired me to not become just another good singer-songwriter, but instead, to become the only Carrie Newcomer, and the truest Carrie Newcomer I could be. One of my own "being true" stories happened to me at about your age. I did not go to college for music. I think when I began college I wasn't ready to risk what I loved the most. I think sometimes we have to get ready to risk what we love, because if it doesn't work out, it will actually mean something. I got a fallback degree in work I enjoyed a lot, visual art. Ok, that tells you a lot about me when my safe and secure fall back plan was visual art. Yes, safe and secure. Visual art, check. Folk singing, check. Eventually I did get a teacher's license so I could teach visual art. But, all through school I was writing songs, and even though I was pretty shy, I began to play music in restaurants and coffeehouses, bars and bowling alleys. I played everywhere, weddings, bat mitzvahs, grocery store openings, I think I even played a few garage sales. And when I graduated from college, music was calling me, songwriting was for me what Parker J. Palmer calls the thing "I couldn't, not do." I had no idea what it would look like. I just knew I had to follow. I had to be true. And after all this time, I'm still following. And, I'm still checking in with my truest heart, and listening closely to what it has to say. I'm still refining my life and work, because of what my true heart tells me. You also have a true heart and a true guide. Breathe deep, and take time to listen – your true heart can be trusted. Keep asking, "How can I bring more of who I am and what I love into my daily life?"

On the way to finding and honoring your truest self, you can be guided by another simple but important practice. Be kind. In your life after Goshen College you will decide not just what you want to "do" in the world, but who you want to "be." You will "do" many things and most likely work a variety of jobs. But in every circumstance, you will choose what kind of spirit you bring to your life and to your work. We talk a lot about love. We talk about love in songs, movies, in spiritual community. Love is big, it's so big and so wide. Sometimes you just can't get your arms around love. But kindness is love in human size. It's the country cousin to love. Kindness brings soup when you're sick, it hangs out in the kitchen washing dishes when no one asked it to, it opens the door when your hands are full, and stops everything to listen to your story. It is not flashy or fancy or likely to make it to the front page. It's a small practice and so humble, it's easy to forget how profoundly powerful it is. Kindness lightens and softens our days. It reframes the world and expresses love on a human scale. This does not mean I've always lived and worked in situations of goodness and light. I had to learn how to navigate in a tough business, particularly for women. But, I made a choice about the kind of spirit that would ground my life and work. Greg Ellison wrote, "I can't change the world, but I can change what is three feet around me." Think about that – no, I can't change the whole world, but I can make a profound difference by choosing what I bring into my daily sphere of influence. I fell in love with my husband, Robert, for many reasons. He's a brilliant man, creative, honest, funny and passionate about his work and activism. And, he's the most kind-hearted man I've ever met. He's an entertainment lawyer and if there was ever a profession that encouraged being the tough guy, well, that would be law. But Robert's approach is fair and respectful. He understands that his clients are sometimes in confusing or anxiety-ridden situations. He's good at what he does, and he gets to "yes" but without the hard edge – and generally, everyone feels better at the end of the process. He honors his own kind heart, and in doing that he shifts something with his every interaction. Think back… remember some small act of kindness extended to you, a kindness that changed something, a kindness you remember to this very day.

When I was a little girl, I went to visit my grandmother Newcomer. Her yard looked like the Garden of Eden and she had planted flowers all round her front porch. I loved my grandmother, and I decided to pick her a bouquet. I remember my mother's horrified face as I held out that bouquet of flowers, bulbs and all. My grandmother did not skip a beat. She just said, "Oh Carrie, what a beautiful bouquet. Thank you. And now, I will teach you how to plant bulbs." Which she did. She did not yell at me, or shame me. She took me by the hand and taught me something very important about how to tend to growing things—like flowers, like relationships, like a child. And to this day, whenever I get my hands in the dirt, whenever I put a bouquet of flowers on the front table, I think of her and that small kindness. The practice of kindness is transformative, and the spirit we chose to bring to our lives and work matters.

The practice of being kind also extends to myself. At 21 years old, I was like many of you here today. I was wise and foolish and beautiful and lost and filled with such good intentions. I was shining. But I did not know it. My time at Goshen College was filled with classes and conversations about what it really meant to live a life of justice and compassion. I believed in the dignity and worth of others, but I didn't yet believe in the depth of my own worthiness. Thomas Merton said, "It cannot be explained. There is no way of telling people that they are all walking around shining like the sun." I wish someone could have told me, "You're all right– you're more than all right – you are shining like the sun." But, I would have to claim that for myself, as you will have to claim that for yourself. Try whenever you can to give yourself the same kindness and encouragement you would give a good friend. The practice of kindness is transformative – in our daily interactions with others, but also in how we befriend ourselves.

A key companion to being true, and being kind is the practice of paying attention. Practice. I love the word "practice," because practice does not imply perfection, it implies intention. I want to be here. I want to show up for my own life. And so I keep practicing. I tell my songwriting students that to write a good story or song you have to be present and pay attention. You can't write a story if you've missed what happened because you were checking your texts. We live in a world of distraction and it's easy, so easy to not be present in our own lives. You have to choose to be present and to notice things. The saddest days of my life are the ones where I get to the end and say, "Dang, I missed it." But be aware that if you are paying attention you'll see things. It's like you make this deal with the universe. I will be here and I will be present. And because of that you will be a different kind of person. You'll probably gasp at sunsets more often. You might weep at a song or sense something extraordinary in what appears to be absolutely ordinary. You might find yourself standing in the middle of the room grinning at something that no one else saw. You'll become the person in the airport who has an invisible sign on your forehead saying "I love a good story" and people will sense this and sit next to you and tell you all kinds of marvelous things. When you are paying attention you will see things, and because of that, you will encounter the good questions. Take notice of these questions, pay attention to the ones that continue to intrigue you, the questions that return, "What do I love beyond words or measure? What sustains me? What does it mean to be true? And when I pull back all the distractions of my life, what is at its very heart?" It is good to have goals and work toward them, but our lives happen here and now. Stay present, take notice and keep asking good questions. I chose to follow music because I was paying attention to what my heart was telling me. What is your heart telling you? I write better songs because I keep showing up. What might you take to a new level if you set an intention to be more present in your own life?

So that's it, three simple human-sized ideas. Be true, be kind, pay attention. Be true, keep checking in with your heart, which is going to take courage at times. Be kind to yourself and to one another. Kindness is love on a human scale. And take notice of how a little kindness can tip the balance toward the light. And finally, pay attention. Be here and aware. This world is a surprising, startling, beautiful place. Don't get to the end of your day, or week, or life and say, "Dang, I missed it." Pay attention to what you love, because love will always take you where you need to go, which is rarely where you expected, but it will be where you need to go.

Thank you for listening to me today. My dear graduates of 2016, you are the glorious next wave. You are shining like the sun. May you know the perfect danger of a beautiful life well lived.

Be True, Be Kind and Pay Attention.

Once You Have Blessed It

John Ames is the main character in the book Gilead by Marilynn Robinson. John is an elderly pastor of a small rural church in Iowa. His son came very late into his life and he knows that he will not live to see his son become a man. In the story, John is writing his son letters and reflections. In one letter he describes how much he loved the ritual of blessing small children. He loved to place his aging palm on their small smooth heads and say the words. He goes on to explain that he did not believe that he was bestowing any holiness or goodness upon the child, but merely affirming and celebrating the holiness already present.

So today as I walked in my beloved woods with my beloved dogs in the beloved newness of springtime, I thought about John Ames and his description of blessing. I was struck by an overwhelming sense of goodness all around me. Could there be a more holy cathedral than a stand of old growth trees? Could there be a greater reminder of the graciousness of the Sacred than the smell of muddy spring earth? I began laying my hands on the sides of trees, offering small blessings as I passed. Bending down, I touched the new green shoots, blessing them as well. I blessed the spring peepers and my very muddy dogs. I blessed last year's leaves in all their many shades of beige. I blessed the clean cold water of the creek. I blessed the Carolina Wren caterwauling from a branch. And just for good measure, I blessed the barred owl that kept me awake last night calling out a haunting blessing of its own. Later, I was in the Woodbridge Station post office mailing a few packages. Standing in line, I found myself silently blessing the Asian student who was obviously confused and yet bravely trying to figure out the nuances of the U.S. postal system. I blessed the harried mother with the toddler on her hip, rocking back and forth and humming a little song. I blessed the grey-haired senior in sensible shoes and the guy on his cell phone. I blessed the tired postal clerk. I found myself blessing every letter and package sent to express love or birthday greetings or just to connect. I blessed it all.

At the end of a day that has been framed by so many blessings my heart felt full and tender. My vision felt kinder and clearer after spending a fair amount of time viewing the natural world and my fellow human beings through the lens of blessedness. In a world of so many sorrows, the act of blessing affirmed that there is still so much that is whole, sacred and good in this world. There is a perceptible shift in any relationship once you have affirmed the holiness that is already present. For once you have blessed anyone or anything, it becomes nearly impossible to see it as completely separate from yourself.

Miracle, Light and Considerable Magic

"Why does this generation ask for a miraculous sign?"
—Mark 8:12

Albert Einstein said, "There are two ways to live your life. One is as though nothing is a miracle. The other is as though everything is a miracle." I know when the world feels anything less than miraculous to me, I'm probably not paying attention. The group of people Jesus was talking to in this gospel story wanted hard evidence of the sacred presence—a flashy, parting-of-the-Red-Sea verification. Jesus responded with a question, inviting them—and us—to reframe what it means to see and experience the living presence. He invited them to think of a miracle as more than a statement punctuated with a period, but rather as part of an ongoing spiritual conversation including many heart-opening questions. How and where does the sacred presence move in our daily lives and world? If I experience a sacred presence within me and all around me, how then shall I live with this knowledge?

As a spiritual songwriter, I often wonder and write about experiencing the mysterious indwelling of the Sacred—in Quakerism referred to as "that of God in everyone" or "The Light"—in ordinary things and daily experiences. Consistently, when I am open to a daily relationship with wonder, wonder usually shows up, or more likely, I finally see what has always been there. I live in southern Indiana, about where the glaciers of the last ice age stopped. It is a rolling green area with deep ravines and lovely deciduous forests. It is also the home to an unusual abundance of a particular kind of stone called the geode. On the outside, geodes look like lumpy grey-brown rocks, but inside they are filled with beautiful quartz crystals. There is a creek that runs through the woods where I live, and it is filled with these amazing rocks. In Monroe County, Indiana, geodes are as common as corn, and yet each one is a wonder. I have a friend from New York that came out to visit me in the wilds of the Midwest. I took her for a walk thinking that we would pick up a few geodes in that creek. She kept looking around saying, "I don't see them. Where are they?" Finally I picked up one, and showed it to her. I said, "See, they look like lumpy, brown brains on the outside." Then she stopped and looked around and said, "Oh my gosh, they're everywhere, they are absolutely everywhere." Now that she had seen the miracle, she could not unsee it.

All these things that we call familiar,
Are just miracles clothed in the commonplace
You'll see it if you try in the next stranger's eyes,
God walks around in muddy boots,
Sometimes rags and that's the truth,
You can't always tell, but sometimes you just know.[1]

When I began sensing the Light in even ordinary things, it changed how I experienced the world, reframing it in a way that counteracted our cultural narrative of lack and replaced it with a wondrous sense of abundance, gratitude and responsibility. I remember taking my daughter to the Monet room at the Art Institute of Chicago when she was five years old. I had shown her postcards of his haystack paintings, explaining that this artist loved the way things looked and felt in different kinds of light and that he used tiny dabs of color to recreate the feelings he loved so much. When we entered the room she stood transfixed, then she ran up to the haystack painting and stood so close to the image that it dissolved into individual strokes. She said, "It's gone. It's just little dots." Then she walked slowly backwards until she was standing next to me, viewing the painting again as a whole. She took my hand and breathed, "There it is. I see it and it's totally made of magic." I said, "Yes, honey, that's how it all works."

---

[1] From "Geodes," by Carrie Newcomer

The world is made of water and dust, ordinary physical things, but all of them are filled with miracle, Light and considerable magic. When I see the world with this frame, small things take on a luminous quality and daily actions become a sacrament. There is no need to wait for a miracle as proof—the miracle we need is already here.

Holy is the dish and drain,
The soap and sink and the cup and plate
And warm wool socks, and the cold white tile,
Showerheads and good dry towels

And frying eggs sound like psalms
With a bit of salt measured in my palm,
It's all a part of a sacrament,
As holy as a day is spent.

Holy is the busy street
And the cars that boom with a passioned beat,
And the checkout girl counting change,
And the hands that shook my hands today.
Hymns of geese fly overhead
And stretch their wings like their parents did
Blessed be the dog that runs in her sleep,
The chase some wild and elusive thing.

Holy is a familiar room
And the quiet moments in the afternoon.
And folding sheets like folding hands,
To pray as only laundry can.
I'm letting go of all I fear,
Like autumn leaves of earth and air.
For summer came and summer went,
As holy as a day is spent.

Holy is the place I stand,
To give whatever small good I can,
And the empty page, the open book,
Redemption everywhere I look.
Unknowingly we slow our pace,
In the shade of unexpected grace,
With grateful smiles and sad lament
As holy as a day is spent.

And morning light sings "Providence"
As holy as a day is spent.[2]

---

[2] From "Holy As the Day Is Spent," by Carrie Newcomer

The True Nature of Knowing

Hank was a retired carpenter, a mystic and a poet. He attended the Bloomington silent Quaker meeting for over fifty years and passed beyond the veil of this world this spring at the age of ninety-five. I always meant to spend more time with Hank. We talked about meeting for coffee or lunch at the Hobnob Corner, but I never followed through. I got to know Hank through sitting together for twenty-four years in the silence of a Quaker meeting for worship. I knew the companionship of his kindred spirit as our souls clasped hands across the room. I knew him through hearing him speak out of the silence in the manner of friends; a brief story or phrase that a person feels pressed to speak out loud to the gathered community. It takes a long time to get a true bead on when to speak and when to be silent in a Quaker Meeting. Eventually most of us learn to listen deeper and speak less. Eventually we experience not trusting our inner voice, deciding not to speak, and realize later we should have. First, you let go of speaking, then you let go of the silence, and then you let go of judgment and have patience with yourself and the process. Over his long years, Hank had learned the art of this kind of patience and discernment. When he stood to speak, we all leaned in. He sensed the unseen world everywhere, especially in the natural world. He caught something luminous from the corner of his eye and would put it into language. He often spoke of an aging oak tree and a red tailed hawk that always seemed to appear in the most meaningful moments. He quoted Whitman and Emerson and his beloved Edna St. Vincent Millay: "O world, I cannot hold thee close enough." He embraced the world, loved the world and could never get it quite close enough. He told circular stories, starting at point A and often visiting B, C, Q and 11 before coming back to A. But I found that if I hung with the story, if I listened with my heart instead of my linear mind, when he finally brought the story back to A, I would sit awash with wonder. It was always the journey I needed to take that day. I heard over the course of twenty-four years, small details of his daily life, large experiences that shaped him. I heard about morning coffee with his wife Mardi. I heard about small shining moments with his daughters and grandchildren. Occasionally, he would speak of his experiences as a conscientious objector in WWII. He had been sent away and interned in several northwestern work camps. They needed the soldiers. Hank was considered dangerous and many believed he was wrong or cowardly. War haunts everyone it touches. There are different kinds of heroes, and more than one kind of courage. I heard the phrases that had followed him for years. I heard the things he felt he knew, and the things he'd still had not figured out. I heard the small nuances of this man's spiritual life shared with humility in a quiet room. After meeting, we often found one another. Often one of us would say to the other, "Friend, you speak to my condition." Which is Quaker shorthand for "Today you spoke what my heart so needed to hear." Sometimes we would chat over an oatmeal cookie, or during an after-meeting potluck. We talked about poetry and our shared love of the mystery of language. Reveling in how poetry works at a slant, inferring what cannot be spoken at all, creating a container for our longings and for all things of shadow and light. I miss him.

In some ways, I'm not sure I could have known him better if I'd had that cup of coffee with him at the Hobnob. But, I think I would have cherished those conversations and that feels like a missed opportunity. But Hank taught me that there are different ways of knowing one another. It was Hank who showed me that I could feel closer to him in the silence then I did with people with whom I spoke every day. I learned that knowing someone primarily through his or her soul's journey is a privilege and incredibly personal. I don't believe that the kind of friendship and knowing that I shared with Hank was greater or lesser than our more common ways of being in a relationship. It is a lateral kind of knowing. We experienced friendship as if it were based in poetry instead of prose, side by side in the quiet, centered in the wordless, the daily and luminous. We were very close friends in the manner of Friends and that has changed forever how I think about speaking and listening and the true nature of knowing.

Another Kind of Flying

"Gravity is a fact everybody knows about. It is always underfoot." —Mary Oliver

Gravity is like our own mortality; both are facts and always a little underfoot. I do not live in a culture that is comfortable acknowledging our own limited time. We are a culture obsessed with youth and the pleasures of youth, as most hedonistic cultures have been. We don't talk about mortality, and those of us who must make meaning and peace with limited time (which is all of us) must often do so alone. Even within our spiritual communities mortality is often relegated to over worn phrases about heavenly reward and glories to come. When someone does speak about limited time and how that might change our approach to daily living we try to "lighten" the conversation. But this lightening is not illumination. It is whitewash. When someone wants a meaningful dialogue about what it means to have lived awhile and how that understanding shifts our priorities and ideas of importance, the tendency is to deal with such attempts as we would a crass, inappropriate comment at a dinner party. We laugh it off then quickly try to distract from the unmannered comment by pointing at some more acceptable bit of tinsel or fluff, gossip, new iPhone models or Donald Trump. But mortality, like gravity, is always pulling us in a direction. If we do not attend to that pull we trip, stumble or just miss the point. Adrienne Rich wrote, "That conversation we were always on the edge of having, runs on in my head."

This is the way of the unsaid thing, the unspoken love, the unnamed fear and the unsung song. We all have songs we were born to sing, always meant to sing. Songs and conversations that were meant to enrich our lives and help us travel with greater awareness and companionship. But when I resist these moments, these intersections of real connection I lose the moment and the song we might have sung together. It takes a long time (if ever) to find a missed moment, to understand what was truly lost and to glean the feathers left behind as the moment flew past us and off into the distance. My mother passed beyond this world when I was in my early 30's. She was a beautiful wounded soul and one of the most private women I've ever known. Of course, who should she birth into her private world but a poet and songwriter, someone who would grow up to say things like, "Let's talk about our feelings...in a song...and now, just for you, in public." She tried her best to deal gracefully with the unmentionable laundry I'd hang out on the backyard clothesline. It made her nervous, but it was my laundry, not hers, and I guess that helped some. I remember sitting with her, the winter light coming through the long living room window of my parents' home. I wanted to ask her about her first kiss, her first car, her most cherished and difficult memories. I wanted to ask her what she had forgiven, and what she would never forgive. I wanted to ask her what she longed for and what she thought mattered, why her favorite color was blue and what she felt about leaving this world with no guarantee of the shape of the next. That afternoon the unsaid words of a lifetime were hanging in the air as thick as pea soup. I remember beginning, braving an unspoken question, and my mother quickly redirecting the conversation to safer, less private territory. If I had been older, I think I would have tried again, taken her hand and said, "I am safe, I love you. I want to know you and to have walked with you, wherever you've been and wherever you are right now." But I pulled back respectfully, folded towels and watched TV and said only, "I love you, Mom" and she said, "I love you too, honey" as feathers gathered in the room, as the last notes of that momentary song faded to a quiet echo.

Another curse of the unsaid is that subject doesn't go away or truly diminish, so we risk having the unspoken overwhelm us with melancholy and anxiety, debilitating us in a variety of ways. After my mother's passing I wrote an inordinate number of songs and poems about her. I tried not to, but whatever I wrote there she was. I finally surrendered to the unsaid and gave myself permission to write about my mother until I felt done. Several years later, long after I'd written all those songs, after I'd concluded I was done and went on to write about other things, I was walking down a busy sidewalk with my teenage daughter. We were talking about classes and her job at the public library, about daily dramas with friends and boys, when she off handedly asked, "If you could do anything you wanted right now, what would you do." Without skipping a beat I said, "I'd talk to my mom." I stopped. Tears immediately pooled and spilled over my eyelids. My daughter was surprised, but not embarrassed and she said, "I love you, Mom," as she pulled a tissue out of her jacket pocket. "I love you too, honey," I returned as I accepted the comfort she offered. I had not realized that the unsaid was that close to the surface, that the unsaid would always be with me even when I was not thinking about it at all.

So gravity and mortality are just facts, always underfoot, but by looking at the said and unsaid, by embracing my limited time, I shift my perspective and priorities. Gravity is not what weighs us down or restrains us from lifting our arms and flying like a broad winged bird. Gravity is what reminds us of our relationship to the ground, to the earth we walk upon. Gravity is also what creates another kind of soaring. It is the triumph of the waterfall, soft, fine mist suspended in air, veils and ribbons of water, sheets of power, falling in a joyous leap of glorious flight. By looking directly at what culturally I am supposed to try to forget, I feel less inclined to be tempted down rabbit holes of distraction and I am more able to embrace my own time here in this messy miraculous world. Yes, gravity and mortality are facts and always underfoot, but perhaps it is also true that our lives are created of suspended moments of glorious flight, one arcing and aching swan dive out and into an endless, welcoming river of time.

- Lyrics -

Lean in Toward the Light

Winter is the oldest season,
But quietly beneath the snow,
Seeds are stretching out and reaching,
Faithful as the morning glow.

Carry nothing but what you must.
Lean in toward the Light.
Let it go, shake off the dust.
Lean in toward the Light.
Today is now, tomorrow beckons.
Lean in toward the Light.
Keep practicing resurrection

The shadows of this world will say,
There's no hope—why try anyway?
But every kindness large or slight,
Shifts the balance toward the light.

Waters wind and open wide.
Lean in toward the Light.
Don't just walk when you can fly.
Lean in toward the Light.
When justice seems in short supply.
Lean in toward the Light.
Let beauty be your truest guide.

The shadows of this world will say,
There's no hope—why try anyway?
But every kindness large or slight,
Shifts the balance toward the light.

The prayer I pray at eventide.
Lean in toward the Light.
All left undone be put aside.
Lean in toward the Light.
And when forgiveness is hard to find,
Lean in toward the Light.
Help me to a least to be kind.
Lean in toward the Light.
Lean in toward the Light.

A Shovel Is a Prayer

"I believe that prayer is very personal and intimate. It happens in small, private moments, in songs and whispers, in humor, grace and the conversations that can only be had at the quiet end of the table." – Carrie Newcomer

A shovel is a prayer
To the farmer's foot
When he steps down
And the soft earth gives way.
A baby is a prayer
When it's finally asleep,
A whispered, "Amen"
At the end of the day.

And a friend is a prayer
When they bring over soup,
When they laugh at your jokes,
And they don't ask for proof.
It's a song that you sing
When you are alone,
When you're weary or lonely
Or that far from home.

For all your searching
There's nothing to do.
What you've been looking for
Is looking for you.

I'm the prodigal daughter,
You're the dissonant son.
We've been washed in rainwater,
We're the fortunate ones.

On the other side of midnight
Just before the dawn,
You can feel it coming up
When the long night is done.

It's as heavy as grief
And its weightless as smoke.
It's the dream you forgot,
It's the letter you wrote,
It's the first birds of morning
That sound like a hymn.
Throw open the windows and
Let the light in.

I'm a wayfaring stranger,
You're Indiana Jones,
We are Gracie and George,
We're Watson and Holmes.
The air is filled with angels.
There's no devil to outrun.
Just sigh and kiss the ground
When the long night is done.

It's a collar turned up,
A kiss on the forehead,
A string and two cans.
It's the last thing you said.
It's a hunch that you follow,
A light in the dark,
An idiot check,
It's a balm for your heart.

For all you searching

There's nothing to do.
What you've been looking for
Is looking for you.

Cedar Rapids 10 AM

A love song

A ceaseless wind blows without mercy,
I pull my jacket tighter.
These boots are old,
But they're still trustworthy
To take me somewhere higher.

Will you come with me to the ridge top?
Lay all your burdens bare,
Right there,
There.

I miss you like a typewriter,
Long and far away.
I love you like an embered fire,
That's warmer than the blaze.

Will you come with me to the ridge top?
Lay all your burdens bare,
Right there,
There.

Take away all the white noise,
It's getting hard to hear.
Souls stretched as thin as tissue paper,
Edged with cuts and tears.

Will you come with me to the ridge top?
Lay all your burdens bare,
Right there,

There.

So much for all the chips we've earned.
So much for all the things we've learned.
So far it is still you and me.

You've always been a cup of coffee,
You've always been the cream.
You've always believed that I was better,
Than I could ever dream.

Will you come with me to the ridge top?
Lay all your burdens bare,
Right there,
There.

The Beautiful Not Yet

We live in an ever accelerating goal-oriented world. It is easy to become distracted and restless. We are not who we were, and yet we are not who we will become. I went for a walk in early spring when the snow was gone but leaves had not yet budded. The light was clear and clean, falling totally unencumbered through the trees. Yes, summer was coming, lush and unsubtle, but in that moment I found myself grateful and in love with the quickening. Life is always lived between then and soon, right here and now, in the beautiful not yet. - Carrie

Spring is humming
Bits of something,
A melody the simple part,
A song that I once knew by heart.

Juniper, wild indigo,
Foxglove, lupine, Queen Anne's lace,
Will be coming any day,

The restlessness,
The quickening,
The almost but
Not yet.

Muddy boots, last year's leaves,
Every spring that came before,
All they were and something more.

The restlessness,
The quickening,
The almost but
Not yet.

Do you see, do you see, do you see it?

Take a breath,
Oh, the restlessness,
The beautiful not yet.

There's a stirring,
There's sweetness,
At the edge of in-between.
I feel it nearly trembling.

The restlessness,
The quickening,
The almost but
Not yet.

Three Feet or So

This song was written for a spoken word and song collaboration with Parker J. Palmer and Gary Walters called "What We Need Is Here: Hope, Hard Times and Human Possibility." I reference in this song a beautiful story by Greg Ellison that affirms the idea that we may not be able to change the whole world, but we can change what is three feet around us. We have enormous power to create positive change in the world in how we choose to live our daily lives.

When I'm weary, lost or sad,
Overwhelmed or just fed up,
I say grace for what I have.
And most the time that is enough.

We are body, skin and bones,
We're all the loss we've ever known,
What is gone is always near,
We're all the love that brought us here.

And the things that have saved us
Are still here to save us.
It's not out there somewhere
It's right here, it's right here.

If I start by being kind,
Love usually follows right behind.
It nods its head and softly hums
Saying, "Honey, that's the way it's done."
We don't have to search for love,
Wring our hands and wring our hearts,
All we have to do is know
The love will find us in the dark

And the things that have saved us
Are still here to save us.
It's not out there somewhere
It's right here, it's right here.

I can't change the whole world.
But I can change the world I know,
What's within three feet or so.

We are body, skin and bones,
We're all the love we've ever known,
When I don't know what is right,
I hold it up into the Light.
I hold it up into the Light.
I hold it up into the Light.

Sanctuary

This song was written after a conversation with my friend Parker J. Palmer. I asked him, "What can we do when we are personally or politically heartbroken?" He responded, "We take sanctuary. We gather with those we love, in places like Brown Chapel. We remember, we share stories or we sit in silence until we can go on."

Will you be my refuge,
My haven in the storm,
Will you keep the embers warm,
When my fire's all but gone?
Will you remember,
And bring me sprigs of rosemary,
Be my sanctuary,
'Til I can carry on
Carry on
Carry on.

This one knocked me to the ground,
This one dropped me to my knees,
I should have seen it coming,
But it surprised me.

Will you be my refuge,
My haven in the storm,
Will you keep the embers warm,
When my fire's all but gone?
Will you remember,
And bring me sprigs of rosemary,
Be my sanctuary,
'Til I can carry on
Carry on

Carry on.
In a state of true believers,
On streets called us and them,
It's gonna take some time,
'Til the world feels safe again.

Will you be my refuge,
My haven in the storm,
Will you keep the embers warm,
When my fire's all but gone?
Will you remember,
And bring me sprigs of rosemary,
Be my sanctuary,
'Til I can carry on
Carry on
Carry on.

You can rest here in Brown Chapel,
Or with a circle of friends,
A quiet grove of trees,
Or between two bookends.

Will you be my refuge,
My haven in the storm,
Will you keep the embers warm,
When my fire's all but gone?
Will you remember,
And bring me sprigs of rosemary,
Be my sanctuary,
'Til I can carry on
Carry on
Carry on.

Help in Hard Times

This is another song written for a song and spoken word collaboration with Parker J. Palmer. I'd like to thank Barbara Brown Taylor for her lovely book Learning to Walk in the Dark. I was very touched by her concept of lunar spirituality. We do not live our lives in full sun or full dark. Our lives are lived more often like the phases of the moon, always incorporating both shadow and light. I've come to believe that there is not always a reason for the hard times we face, but I do believe in those difficult moments there is help and hope. Even when the moon is dark, there is still something whole and sacred in the world.

I am learning to walk with grace in the dark.
I am learning to trust and to lead with my heart.
When the old moon is gone into silence and sighs,
It's the one and only time a new moon can rise.

Sometimes there is no reason, the moon waxes and wanes,
It was the 100-year flood and you were in the way.
Some things we find in daylight and we're grateful to know.
Some things we only learned where we did not want to go.

I can't tell you it will all turn out fine,
But I know is there is help in hard times.

Bruised and bewildered I am looking out the door,
Unsure of how to do what I've never done before.
But I am not alone, with my questions and my fears,
When the old moon is done, the new moon appears.

I'm inspired and troubled by the stories I have heard.
In the blue light of evening all boundaries get blurred.
And I believe in something better, and that love's the final word,
And that there's still something whole and sacred in this world.

I can't tell you it will all turn out fine,
But I know is there is help in hard times.

Sure it could, it could all be just fine
But I know there is help in hard times.
All I know is there's help in hard times.
All I know is there's help in hard times.

The Season of Mercy

This song began as a poem written while traveling on a train from Berlin to Hannover Germany.

Traveling north,
Tall straight pines,
Ghost white birch
On the Hannover Line.

Red tile roofs,
A lone blue kite,
It's barely tethered
In the silver light.

It's the time of memory
The season of mercy.
Following out the thread,
Humming the tune in my head
Just out of reach,
Always out of reach.

Entering radio silence.
In a train car of sound,
Two dark-eyed children,
Look up and then down.

You buy a strong coffee,
I consider the miles.
Will I be remembered
As the woman who smiled?

It's the time of memory,

The season of mercy.
Following out the thread,
Humming the tune in my head
Just out of reach,
Always out of reach.

How much did I miss or forget to remember,
Here at the edge of November,
With all we've gained and lost?
Do I love my life enough to brave it,
Do I love my life enough to save it?
Where does this train stop?

A red tail hawk
Makes a perfect arc.
A silent owl,
Glides in the dark.

The car fills with light.
That was all that it took.
It was already there
Before I thought to look.

Its the time of memory,
The season of mercy.
Following out the thread,
Humming the tune in my head
Just out of reach,
Always out of reach.
Always out of reach.

You Can Do This Hard Thing

Barbara Kingsolver speaks about a phrase she uses to encourage her children, "You can do hard things." I loved this idea behind this phrase. It absolutely acknowledges the difficulty of the task at hand, and yet, at the same time it completely affirms that the child has everything they need to move forward, and that there is support for them as they move forward. I began to think about all the times in my own life that someone has given me that kind of sound advice and encouragement. This is another song written for a spoken word and song collaboration with Parker J. Palmer.

There at the table
With my head in my hands.
A column of numbers
I just could not understand.
You said "Add these together,
Carry the two,
Now you."

You can do this hard thing.
You can do this hard thing.
It's not easy I know,
But I believe that it's so.
You can do this hard thing.

At a cold winter station
Breathing into our gloves.
This would change me forever
Leaving for God knows what.
You carried my bags,
You said, "I'll wait
For you."

You can do this hard thing.

You can do this hard thing.
It's not easy I know,
But I believe that it's so.
You can do this hard thing.

Late at night I called,
And you answered the phone.
The worst it had happened,
And I did not want to be alone.
You quietly listened,
You said, "We'll see this through."

You can do this hard thing.
You can do this hard thing.
It's not easy I know,
But I believe that it's so.
You can do this hard thing.

Here we stand breathless
And pressed in hard times.
Hearts hung like laundry
On backyard clotheslines.
Impossible just takes
A little more time.

From the muddy ground
Comes a green volunteer.
In a place we thought barren
New life appears.
Morning will come whistling
Some comforting tune
For you.

You can do this hard thing.
You can do this hard thing.
It's not easy I know,
But I believe that it's so.
You can do this hard thing.

Where the Light Comes Down

In the beautiful poem "Monet Refuses the Operation" by Lisel Mueller, the French Impressionist painter Claude Monet tells the eye doctor that he does not want the cataract surgery that would restore his eyes. He says it took an entire lifetime to learn to see the world as he does now. What the doctor considers an affliction is actually the outcome of long work and effort. It takes a long time to see the world as mostly made of light and to sense ache and awe at every turn. It takes practice, forgetting and remembering to learn how to pay attention to small things. There is great reward as well as a cost to living such a life. But for the painter, it could not have been any other way.

It took dog days and years,
To catch a moment when it's here.
And that the hay bales just might,
Be mostly made of light,
And that leaves can fall like shining golden coins.

I can feel it in the hollow spaces
In the quiet places
Where the light comes down.
I can see it in strangers' faces,
In the lines and traces,
on the winter ground,
Where the light comes down.

It took awhile before I saw,
That the world is mostly made of ache and awe.
And that some nights hum with sound,
And sometimes silence is a noun,
And that dust and snow can swirl like falling scarves.

I can feel it in the hollow spaces
In the quiet places

Where the light comes down.
I can see it in strangers' faces,
In the lines and traces,
on the winter ground,
Where the light comes down.

Ashes fall and waters rise.
Seasons change before our eyes.

It took a while to finally know
That a Luna moth will quickly come and go,
And that distraction is a thief
Of all that's shining and brief,
Gone in a brilliant startle of wings.

Haunted

Our cultural relationship to mental health has improved greatly in the past generation. And yet, there is still a long way to go toward acknowledgment and acceptance of mental health issues. There are hauntings that have followed us for years: and the whispers of what happened continue to echo.

I've been hearing footsteps on the stairs,
Flip on the light and no one's there.
This is how we learn to navigate
All ghosts and lingering wraiths.

The things you try to hide will not be hid,
They said it didn't happen, but it did.
All the things that scared you as a kid,
In the basement, underneath the bed.

Haunted

If you look long into the dark,
Something will illuminate or spark.
If you wade where the silence is deep,
If you listen long enough it speaks.

Not every haunting is redeemed,
But not every ghost is what it seems.
When we name the dragons, dragons fall,
Armored flanks, flaming wings and all.

Haunted

It's calling through the keyholes,
Underneath the doors,

Slipping through the windows and floorboards.

Shameful stories, unmet needs,
Old ideas and even older deeds,
It's safe to finally release
The shadows of all these.

It's dangerous to live in a normal world,
When you're not an ordinary girl.
For years in dusty attics you could find
Where the mad and voiceless were confined.

Haunted.

The Slender Thread

There is a thread that connects me to the people I love. It has always been that thread I follow to find my way home.

The car wheels hummed and the radio whined,
The rise and fall of telephone lines.
I was trying to remember the last thing you said,
Holding on to the slender thread.

I was awakened last night by the knife of a moon,
I've been spooling out a thread from my heart to you.
Don't give up on me whatever you do,
I'm holding on to the slender thread.

So look up and bless every guiding star,
We've worked so hard and come so far.
And home is still wherever you are,
Holding on to the slender thread.

I never knew it would come to this
That world I knew would no longer exist.
I can still feel it burn like a place you kissed
Holding on to the slender thread.

So look up and bless every guiding star,
We've worked so hard and come so far.
And home is still wherever you are,
Holding on to the slender thread.

Scams and scriptures posted by the roadside.
Whole stories hung out on loose on the clotheslines.
I've left a trail of crumbs and a paper map,

As the miles unravel, it's love that calls me back.

I used to lay out altars in hotel rooms,
On cigarette-burnt tables, and check out at noon.
A stone and a feather and a letter from you,
Holding on to the slender thread.

So look up and bless every guiding star,
We've worked so hard and come so far.
And home is still wherever you are,
Holding on to the slender thread.

- Acknowledgements -

Credits & Appreciation

In great appreciation to my husband, Robert Meitus. Thank you for believing always in the weight and worth of my songs, poetry and stories.

Many thanks to my friends and family for their encouragement and for reading many of these pieces while they were in process.

Thank you to my editor, Cate Whetzel, and to Tim Gaskins at Available Light Publishing for beautifully designing this book.

Made in the USA
San Bernardino, CA
05 October 2016